*The*

HEDGEHOG HANDBOOK

# THE
# HEDGEHOG
# HANDBOOK

*Sally Coulthard*

HEAD
*of* ZEUS

An Anima Book

This book was first published in the UK in 2018 by Anima
This paperback edition published in 2019 by Anima,
an imprint of Head of Zeus Ltd

9 7 5 3 1 2 4 6 8

A catalogue record for this book is available from
the British Library.

ISBN (PB): 9781789545876
ISBN (E): 9781788541121

Typeset by Lindsay Nash
Illustrations by Vanessa Lubach
Illustrations pp 27 and 100-101 by Sylvie Rabbe

Printed and bound in Great Britain
by CPI Group (UK) Ltd, Croydon CR0 4YY

Head of Zeus Ltd
First Floor East
5–8 Hardwick Street
London EC1R 4RG
www.headofzeus.com

For Jane

# CONTENTS

# INTRODUCTION

We're a nostalgic bunch. Ask anyone over thirty and they'll always tell you that when they were kids, the summers were hotter, people were friendlier and it always snowed at Christmas. Probably not true, but memories have a habit of playing tricks on you.

But what about when people say they never see hedgehogs any more? Was there really a time when our gardens were regularly visited by our prickly friends? The sad fact is that, despite our propensity for rose-tinted glasses, there *were* more hedgehogs around when we were children. While most adults can remember a childhood visit from a real Mrs Tiggy-Winkle, few kids today have had the pleasure of coming face-to-face with a hedgehog.

And it's not just that there are fewer hedgehogs than there were. It's estimated that in the 1950s there were around thirty million hedgehogs in the

UK. Now, the best guess is that we're down to *less than a million*. It's something of an understatement to say that not all is as it should be.

But the aim of this book is not to make you feel hopeless. Far from it. This is a book designed to do two things. The first is to give you a quick glimpse into the habits and lifestyle of one of the most enigmatic wild creatures we know. Hedgehogs are fascinating, there's no getting round it. From their night-time routines to their noisy eating, they're full of character, vim and rambling charm. With their quiet determination and bristling, bumbling ways, they're one of the most enduring symbols of the countryside and a traditional, rural way of life. This shy, shuffling animal has captured the imagination of children and grown-ups for centuries, from the timeless stories of Beatrix Potter to modern Instagram sensations such as Biddy the Hedgehog, an African pygmy pet hedgehog with his half a million followers (now sadly deceased, RIP).

But there's also a good reason to know more about hedgehogs – only once we understand their nature and biology can we work out what's going wrong and, hopefully, fix it. It's not helpful to talk about hedgehogs being extinct in five, ten, fifteen years' time – not only does it give that outcome an air of inevitability but, more importantly, we simply *don't know* what's going to happen. The focus needs to be on helping hedgehogs cope with changed circumstances (i.e. a landscape that's not as hedgehog-friendly as it once was) and doing positive things that help existing hedgehog populations to carry on life as normally as possible (such as creating hedgehog highways and encouraging wilder, more natural areas in gardens).

So, the book takes you through a year in a hedgehog's life, starting in spring, when she wakes from a long winter's hibernation. Woven throughout this narrative you'll find practical advice on how to help hedgehogs in your own neighbourhood, and more information about their habits, biology and life cycle. If you've picked up this book there's a good chance you're already hooked on hedgehogs. If not, you should be. There's a growing army of conservationists, volunteers and like-minded people who are passionate about preserving our prickly friend – and we always need more recruits...

3

# MARCH

*It's March, at last. Winter has loosened her icy grip and there are signs that spring is slowly emerging. Primroses and bluebell leaves push their way through the woodland floor, early bumblebees hum along the clearings, and in the trees rooks repair their unruly nests, shouting as they go.*

Like keen shoppers at a spring sale, a handful of creatures are making the most of these lenient days after a long, hard winter. Courting hares fist fight in the open fields. Badgers scramble out of their setts while the cubs snooze underground. Even the odd brimstone butterfly, with his buttery wings, has been seen circling the air after months of ivy-covered sleep.

Come the dusk and, at the bottom of a blackthorn hedge, the tip of a snout appears from a pile of leaves, sniffing the air. It's a hedgehog, woken from three months of enforced isolation, and she's hungry.

The leafy nest has insulated her from the worst excesses of winter but she's also acutely attuned to any changes in the outside temperature. The last few days have been warmer, less hostile, and triggered her wake-up phase – a gentle 'coming to' from an entire season of suspended animation; barely breathing, immobile and cold to the touch.

*She's thin. During hibernation, she's lost over a third of her body weight and needs to build up her strength quickly. And so, with the thought of a fat slug or juicy worm whetting her appetite, she shuffles out into the night...*

## The Hedgehog

The English like to think they invented the hedgehog. And, in a funny way, they did. Travel back six hundred years, to the Middle Ages, and you find the first recorded instance of the word – *hygehoge* – a simple marriage of 'hyge' (hedge) and 'hoge' (pig). It was a straightforward, no-nonsense name – did exactly what it said on the tin – and described the creature perfectly: a snuffling, grunting, hog-snouted beastie that liked nothing better than hanging around hedgerows.

The name stuck. And describes the European hedgehog (*Erinaceus europaeus*) to a T. But nature is never that straightforward. There are, in fact, over fifteen different species of hedgehog scattered across the globe and some of them are not even that hedge-loving. Hedgehogs belong to a family called *Erinaceinae*, a group of mammals that can be found in terrain as diverse as arid desert, open savannah and lush woodland, and vary in colour from white albino to nearly black.

Despite their spines, hedgehogs share more in common, taxonomically speaking, with shrews and moles than other similar prickly mammals such as porcupines, and the European hedgehog is the biggest species of them all – averaging between 450 grams and 1.2 kilograms (1–2½ lb), although you do occasionally see the odd 2-kilogram (4½ lb) whopper. At the other end of the spectrum, there are also some tiddlers – the African pygmy, for example, the species most commonly kept as a pet, can weigh as little as 200 grams (7 oz) and fits neatly into a teacup.

For all their differences, however, most species of hedgehog share some extraordinary traits that set them apart from other mammals. The first, of course, is their spines. Somewhere along the evolutionary line, hedgehogs decided to forgo the warmth of thick fur and opted, instead, for a coat of armour. The spines are hollow hairs, stiffened with keratin, the protein that also makes nails, hooves and horns. It was a canny move – few animals will brave five thousand inch-long needles for a quick meal, so the hedgehog is largely left in peace.

Their spines aren't everywhere, however. A hedgehog's face, legs and belly are, instead, covered in short, coarse fur. These are the vulnerable bits, and so the second of the hedgehog's extraordinary traits is the unique defence mechanism that when under threat,

it pulls itself into a ball, like a drawstring washbag, tucking its head, tail and legs in for protection. Only animals that have powerful enough claws to prise a hedgehog open, like the badger, can break through such an effective, two-pronged defence mechanism.

But prickles come at a cost and offer little protection against the cold, which brings us nicely to their third most recognizable trait – hibernation. European hedgehogs hibernate over winter – usually between December and March, depending on the weather. They do this not just to cope with extremes in temperature, but also because their main food supply, creepy crawlies, largely disappears for the winter. But more about hibernation later.

Hedgehogs are also nocturnal. It's not unheard of for hedgehogs to be out during daylight hours – but it's unusual and often an indication that's something's amiss. Domesticated hedgehogs are also, in theory, nocturnal but have been known to adapt to handlers' daytime routines or live a crepuscular existence, enjoying the twilight hours of dusk and dawn.

As creatures of the night, it's perhaps not surprising that their senses of smell, taste and hearing are highly attuned. When you prowl around in pitch darkness, a smell or sound will catch your attention where a visual cue will fail. But it's not true that hedgehogs have poor eyesight – research into the anatomy of a hedgehog's eye has shown that, in good light, hedgehogs have pretty good sight and may even see in limited colour. The fact is that hedgehogs don't use their eyes because they don't *need* to.

---

### DID YOU KNOW
*Hedgehogs can climb trees and swim.*

---

Just as for many night-time patrollers, life is a solitary affair. Hedgehogs are loners; apart from a brief spell with mother, and a rushed courtship, hedgehogs live happily by themselves, snoozing by day in makeshift nests and heading out into the darkness for an evening of wandering and munching.

One strange piece of behaviour that hedgehogs exhibit is something called 'self-anointing'. Hedgehogs can spend anything from a few minutes to several hours covering their spines in frothy saliva, an act that keeps them so engrossed they barely notice their surroundings. It's not entirely clear why they do it – strong smells and tastes often trigger an episode – but it may be something to do with scent-marking or attracting a sexual partner, males lathering themselves up most frequently during the mating season.

# Hedgehog Habitat

Hedgehogs only really need two things to be happy: something to eat and somewhere to sleep. Thankfully, the British countryside has, until recently, provided both in abundance.

For centuries, the country has been a patchwork of rough pasture, woodlands and hedgerows. These rich and varied environments are filled with the things hedgehogs love – beetles, slugs and worms – and cosy nesting opportunities such as piles of leaves, fallen logs and brambly scrubland.

But the countryside is changing. People want cheap food. The population is also growing and needs more space. It's a big ask and the only way to do this, it seems, is to make the land work harder. We now see larger, more intensively farmed fields, less diversity, more agrichemicals and fewer ancient hedgerows – the traditional stomping ground of the hedgehog is fast disappearing and, crucially, fragmenting. Add to this busier roads, less native woodland and an increase in housing development, and it's easy to see why the hedgehog is struggling.

Estimates vary but Britain had roughly thirty million hedgehogs in the 1950s. New evidence suggests that we're now down to less than a million. That's a crushing reduction in anyone's book.

But nature is no slouch and hedgehogs are attempting to adapt to new circumstances. While the countryside becomes less diverse and large arable fields offer fewer opportunities, suburbia is becoming something of a refuge. City gardens and green spaces such as cemeteries, railway embankments and parks can provide hedgehogs with rich pickings. Urban life is surprisingly biodiverse, with a select range of insects on the menu and other hedgehoggy treats such as birds' eggs, carrion and pet food. Tummies full, hedgehogs also find that the bright lights of city

DID YOU KNOW

*A quarter of people have never seen a hedgehog in their garden.*

SOURCE: RSPB

living provide lots of sleeping opportunities, making their nests tucked under sheds, in compost heaps and hiding in piles of leaf litter. It's not ideal, but needs must.

# APRIL

*April blows in. And it feels as if the countryside is finally shaking off the last vestiges of a long, cold winter. The warmer weather heralds a new invasion: hosts of migrating birds, thousands of miles from their winter home, pour in. Swallows and martins fill the skies, soon followed by the nightingale and cuckoo, crossing paths with the outgoing parties – swans, geese and wading birds – who are on their way further north.*

The once-naked trees are leafing up, like
gentlemen putting on their green cloaks, one,
politely, after the other: first the elder, horse
chestnut, larch and birch, with oak and
ash soon following suit.

Blossom is everywhere. It's a spring white
wedding in the verges – wild cherry,
blackthorn, then the hawthorn, falling like
confetti at the slightest touch. Wrens are
in full voice, the boys singing for attention,
building nests to attract a prospective wife
with her clutch of tiny eggs.

And during these damp April nights, the
hedgehog is busy, travelling far and wide
in search of food. Males will wander further,
two or three kilometres in one evening
(½–1 mile), but the female will stay closer to
her stomping ground, venturing only
a kilometre or so (½ mile) in one sojourn.
A nomad, constantly on the move, she may
only stay for a few days in one nest,
preferring to move on to pastures new,

*hoovering up mouthfuls of newly
emerged baby slugs, earthworms and
leatherjackets as she goes.*

## Hedgehog Diet

Hedgehogs are noisy, enthusiastic eaters. Like greedy toddlers, they eat with deliciously few table manners – plenty of crunching, open-mouthed slurping and lip-smacking going on with every meal.

Like all good eaters, hedgehogs pick from a wide menu – they're generalists, surviving on a diet consisting largely of insects. This unfussy palate serves hedgehogs well; not only will they devour slugs, earwigs, beetles and worms with relish, but they can also stomach caterpillars and millipedes which, to other species, taste bitter or unpleasant. Slug mucus, which puts off many potential predators, is no match for our prickly friend – hedgehogs have even been seen rolling slugs on the ground prior to devouring them, to remove their unpalatable slime, and studies show that bee venom, wasp stings and ant bites also fail to raise a hoggy eyebrow.

Studies of hedgehog droppings have also shown they'll eagerly try spiders, butterflies, flies, young woodlice (older ones secrete a nasty chemical) and snails – like a hipster foodie following what's available season to season. Hedgehogs also love meat and will often munch away on the decaying flesh of other small animals, baby mice, ground-nesting chicks, birds' eggs, frogs, lizards and, occasionally, fallen fruit, seeds and berries (although it's not entirely

## DID YOU KNOW

*Hedgehogs have more teeth than humans – between 36 and 44 (humans have only 32).*

clear whether they can actually absorb any nutrients from fruit and vegetables).

It's difficult to know exactly how much hedgehogs eat in one sitting – it depends on the availability of food and how hungry the hedgehog is. In one night's foraging, however, a hedgehog can easily scoff 50–70 grams (2–3 oz) of food – and when you consider that the average garden slug weighs less than a gram, it's easy to see why hedgehogs need to travel long distances to find enough ingredients to make a meal.

In the wild, a hedgehog's diet is high in protein and low in fat. This, combined with a generous night-time walking regime, ensures that most hedgehogs are fighting fit. In fact, being underweight is more often the issue – the months leading up to hibernation are often a frantic food grab for hedgehogs in an attempt to reach a healthy enough weight to survive the winter. There's no precise hibernation weight that will ensure survival – different regions have shorter or longer winters – but wildlife groups usually agree that any hedgehog less than

450 grams (1 lb) will struggle to go the distance until March.

For pet species and rescued hedgehogs, however, obesity can be an issue. Lack of exercise and over-feeding has led to some hedgehogs being so fat they can't even roll into a ball (the hedgehog equivalent of not being able to put your socks on). There's lots of advice for pet hedgehog owners online but it's clear that, as for many animals (including us), the route to a healthy hedgehog weight is lower calorie intake and more exercise.

The wild hedgehog's diet is also rich in a substance called *chitin* – which comes from the hard shells of insects and helps a hedgehog's digestion by acting like roughage. It's absent in cat and dog food – which can play a large part in a pet hedgehog's diet – so to avoid hedgehog tummy troubles you need to add chitin supplements to their diet.

Some well-meaning rescuers and pet owners also give dried mealworms as a treat – the jury's out on how good these are for hedgehogs. On the one hand, hedgehogs *love* them and they naturally contain plenty of chitin; on the other, they're thought to cause calcium depletion and bone problems if eaten in any quantity. The advice most rescue centres now give is to treat mealworms like bags of crisps – fine for the occasional snack, but only as part of a balanced diet.

## *Help a Hedgehog No. 1*

### PUT FOOD OUT IN THE GARDEN

The only time hedgehogs don't think about food is when they're asleep. They're either fattening up after a long period in hibernation, keeping up their energy levels for the breeding season, or desperately putting on weight in time for winter again. It's a constant battle to find enough insects to eat, especially when gardens are over-manicured or hedgerows thin on the ground.

So, whether you live in the countryside or an inner city, putting out food for hedgehogs is a sure-fire way to help them through any lean periods. Research shows that feeding hedgehogs can increase their chances of survival without affecting their natural behaviour – in other words, you won't ruin their foraging instincts with supplementary feeding.

### WHAT TO FEED HEDGEHOGS

Cat food or dog food (tinned or biscuits), minced meat, chopped boiled eggs, specialist hedgehog food (Spike's Dinner or Ark Hedgehog Original), and plenty of fresh water. For one hedgehog, 100 grams (3½ oz) of food per night is enough, but you can always put out more if you think you're getting multiple visitors.

## WHAT *NOT* TO FEED HEDGEHOGS

Contrary to what we were told as children, hedgehogs must *not* be given milk. Hedgehogs are lactose intolerant and dairy products will give them diarrhoea. Bread, cakes, sweet biscuits and salty processed foods like crisps don't do them any good either, so avoid.

## HOW TO FEED HEDGEHOGS

Leave any food in a shallow dish and put it in the same place, in a sheltered part of your garden, just before dusk. Put water in a separate shallow bowl – hedgehogs tend to tip things over easily, so a heavy-bottomed dish is best. In the morning, remove any leftover food.

## WHEN TO FEED HEDGEHOGS

Between March and December, put food out every day if you can. Once hedgehogs start coming into your garden, they'll often return night after night. If you go away on holiday, leave dry pet biscuits and water out. During hibernation – December to March – hedgehogs are asleep but may still wake up and need a quick snack. A ready supply of water and dry biscuits can be a life-saver, especially if the ground is frozen.

## HOW TO MAKE A FEEDING STATION

If you want to stop pets or other animals eating the food you put out for hedgehogs, or to keep off the rain, make a simple feeding station from a plastic storage box (see opposite). Check it every day and replace the food and water daily. Another brick 13 centimetres (5 in) from the entrance can prevent cats from lying down and hooking out the food.

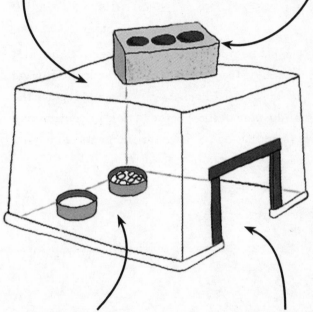

25L clear plastic storage box, upside down

Brick on top to stop it being blown or tipped over

Water and food in separate bowls at far end of the box

Cut out 4 inch x 4 inch hole. Gaffer tape over the sharp edges

# MAY

*May, and the countryside is more alive than ever. Spring, now well into her stride, has revealed fields and verges foaming with cow parsley, creamy buttercups and wild strawberries.*

*The dawn chorus is at its finest. The early risers, an hour before the sun comes up, ignore the chill air and start the proceedings – the skylarks, song thrushes and blackbirds – all in fine voice. A little later, the stragglers to the party, the wrens and warblers, join the medley.*

*It's a fine time to sing. The countryside is otherwise silent so early in the day, helping the birdsong carry far on the morning breeze. It's also too early for breakfast – the darkness making it tricky to find a meal – so what better way to spend the first moments of the day than singing for a mate.*

*And it's not just the birds who are looking for company. Only a few hours before sunrise, a strange dance was taking place in the darkness. Our hedgehog, ready to mate but slow to give up her virtue, has spent an exhausting evening rebuffing the attention of an enthusiastic suitor. His attempts to charm her with endless circling, snorting and*

*puffing didn't initially meet with a warm
reception. It's been a long-winded evening of
playing hard to get, but fortune, it seems,
favours the persistent...*

## Finding a Mate

There's an old joke, 'How does a hedgehog mate' – the answer, of course, being 'Very carefully'.

The whole business of hedgehog courtship and sex has, until recently, been little understood. Aristotle thought that the only way two such spiky creatures could possibly mate would be belly to belly and it's easy to see why there'd be room for confusion – thanks to their nocturnal lifestyles, hedgehogs are rarely seen *in flagrante*, and even if you do manage to catch a pair of hedgehogs in action, it's jolly tricky to see what's going on under all those prickles.

From anecdotal evidence and small studies, however, it's clear that hedgehogs aren't the most romantic of creatures. Far from pair-bonding for life, and the male sticking around to help rear the young, it seems the hedgehog's sex life is one long, gloriously promiscuous Freshers' Week of clumsy advances and multiple partners.

Hedgehogs can breed from April right through until September but it's the month of May that sees the most amorous, frenzied period of mating known as the 'rut'. Both sexes will have been out of hibernation for weeks and, hopefully, back to a normal weight. Night-time grub hunts are still a priority, but now come with the added thrill – for the male at least – of no-strings sex.

It all begins with the male hedgehog catching the scent of a female in heat. All thoughts of searching for food are abandoned in favour of sniffing out the object of his affections. When he finds her, he knows he must impress her. A 'dance' ensues: he circles her endlessly, snorting and grunting, pointing his nose in her direction. It's a noisy affair and one that often attracts unwanted attention from rival males nearby. Like so many youthful evenings, it can all end in tears – a bar-room brawl of head butting, charging and chasing, while the female hedgehog wanders off unnoticed.

For those females who choose to stick around, they abide by only one relationship philosophy: treat them mean, keep them keen. Far from being impressed by the male's courtship display and general thuggery, the female's initial reaction is to respond aggressively, bristling her spines and turning her flank to face him. Time and time again the male will walk in a ring around her, huffing and puffing, only to receive the cold shoulder.

But that's all part of the plan. His war of attrition demonstrates just what a great mate he'll make – dogged persistence shows he's a tough partner. Only one in ten of these courtship dance-offs ends in sex, so the male hedgehog will play the numbers game, approaching as many females as he can find until one lucky lady says yes.

When she does give in, there's the small matter of five thousand spines. Her trick is to flatten her posture and spikes, allowing the male to

mount without impaling himself. It's a delicate oper-
ation but thankfully brief – a few rapid thrusts and
it's all over.

There's no time for pillow talk. Both parties go
their separate ways. And unlike some species, where
the male will guard the female to prevent any further mating from rivals, the male hedgehog quickly
wanders off without a backward glance. What's
more, both parties will have numerous more sexual
encounters before the season, if not the night, is
out. (The male hedgehog does secure his advantage,
however, with something rather nifty – he 'plugs' the
female's vagina with his sperm, blocking the passage
for any later suitors. Moles, bees, kangaroos and
scorpions also use the same trick.) Oh, the romance
of it all.

# Help a Hedgehog No. 2

## CREATE WILDLIFE CORNERS

Hedgehogs are travellers. They might sleep in the same spot for a few days on the trot but they're wanderers at heart, and wherever they lay their spikes, that's their home.

They walk huge distances – often 2 kilometres (1¼ miles) a night – and cover a wide area. This itinerant lifestyle means they constantly need to find new places to sleep that are quiet, hidden and overgrown – not easy in a smart garden or ploughed field. And come hibernation, the pressure to find a secluded corner becomes even greater.

But you can help. Creating wild areas in the garden, however small, allows hedgehogs to rest in the day and roam freely for food and mates at night.

- Don't clear away all the **leaf litter**. Push a pile of fallen leaves into a quiet corner of the garden – it'll make the perfect day nest.

- Create a permanent **log stack** or mound of twigs. Hedgehogs will crawl into the tight spaces underneath and it'll provide a welcome source of bugs.
- Leave an **overgrown patch**. Let a space in your garden become wild and unruly – hedgehogs will find food and shelter in long grass, scrub and brambles.
- Plant **hedgerows** – if you need to replace a boundary or wall, plant a mixed hedge instead. Wooden fences offer little for wildlife but a hedge will provide shelter and food for hedgehogs and

for the dozens of insects, birds and mammals that visit your garden. Try to include several different species of plant in the same hedge – that way they'll leaf up, flower and fruit at different points during the year. If you do have to use a solid fence, see Creating Hedgehog Highways, page 87.

# JUNE

*Early summer floats in on a warm breeze.
It's June and the countryside is awash with
colour and perfume. The tree canopies,
heavy with leaves, cast shade onto
the woodland floor, but out in the sunlit
hedgerows, wild flowers – dog roses,
honeysuckle and elderflowers –
scramble for attention.*

*The nights are now short and mild. Come the dusk and many of nature's nocturnal animals will already be out, making up for lost time. Pipistrelle bats zip back and forth, barn owls haunt the woodland edges and rough grassland, and moths, in their hundreds, flit around the porch lights, charmed to distraction.*

*At the base of a thick bramble bush, the hedgehog is busy making a maternity nest. It's four weeks since the mating. She's heavily pregnant and about to give birth to her hoglets. Time is short – and she's even been out in daylight hours – but it's vital she's prepared. Grabbing mouthfuls of leaves and moss from the surrounding verge, she dashes back and forth under the criss-crossed twigs, plumping the nest with each visit.*

*It's more luxurious than her usual day nests – on most days she's happy enough snuggling under a loose pile of leaves –*

*but this birthing house needs to be cosy,*
*well covered and robust. Once the babies are*
*born, she'll stay with them for the next*
*month or two, until she's confident they can*
*make it alone. But that's weeks away. First,*
*there's the small matter of labour and*
*multiple births to get through...*

## Hedgehog Birth and Babies

While hedgehogs will breed and have babies through-out the summer months, June is the busiest time for new arrivals. After the madness of the May 'rut', the male hedgehog has no further involvement, leaving the female to carry, birth and raise the youngsters alone.

Gestation is only four to five weeks, so it's not long after mating that the female hedgehog starts to show signs of pregnancy and begins the task of building a maternity nest. She'll put on weight, feeding as often as possible, while finding a suitable site for her brief confinement.

It needs to be quiet, and well concealed, so she might choose an old burrow or space under a shed. Hedges and thick bushes are also favourite nesting sites, and there she'll give birth, one by one, to a handful of tiny, smooth-skinned babies known as hoglets.

If the weather takes a turn for the worst, and there's a prolonged cold snap, the female can do something extraordinary and go into mini-hibernation, metaphorically pressing the 'pause button' on her pregnancy. The development of the embryos slows down until the good weather returns and she wakes up from her torpor.

Hedgehogs can have up to ten or more hoglets,

but it's rare, most litters consisting of just four or five babies. The hoglets are born blind and, blessedly, spike-free. It's a neat trick – the skin of the new hoglet is saturated with fluid – rather like a blister – preventing the spines underneath from poking through. Just hours after delivery, this fluid will be reabsorbed, allowing the spikes to erupt through the skin. The first spikes are white, and only a few hundred in number. It's not until a few days later that the stiffer, brown spines start to appear and soon cover the growing hoglet in its characteristic coat of armour.

For the first few weeks the baby hedgehogs will need only their mother's milk. Like a cat with kittens, she'll lie on her side, allowing the row of hoglets to drink greedily. She has three pairs of nipples – enough for six hoglets but no more. It's draining work, feeding, and the mother will still need to eat to keep up her strength – the soft peeping of contented hoglets soon turns to loud squalls when she shifts position or leaves the nest to forage for insects.

In fact, early summer is often one of the few times when you'll see healthy hedgehogs out in daylight

## DID YOU KNOW

*Baby hedgehogs are called hoglets. They're also known as piglets, pups or kittens.*

hours. In normal circumstances, hedgehogs only forage at night, but busy mums will often steal a few extra hours in the daytime to hunt for food while the hoglets are asleep. Female hedgehogs may also be outside if they're building a maternity nest or moving their babies to a new location if the nest is damaged.

If you do see a hedgehog out in the summer and it has a purposeful spring in its step, leave it be. If it's got a mouthful of leaves it's almost certainly building a maternity nest. If it's carrying a baby in its mouth, it's moving home in a hurry. Let her get on her way but, if possible, leave some food and water out nearby. If a hedgehog is moving strangely, however, dragging an injured limb, wobbling, 'sunbathing' or sleeping out in the open, then something's wrong and it'll need assistance (see Sick or Injured Hedgehogs, page 54, and Rescuing Orphaned Hoglets, page 63).

The birth is a vulnerable time, as are the first few weeks after. If the nest is disturbed or a male hedgehog finds his way inside, it can spell disaster: a stressed mother will abandon or even eat her hoglets. It's not clear why hedgehog mothers do this – and not unheard of in other species – but there are a number of possible theories.

If food is scarce, a mother may eat some or all of her young as a way of ensuring that whoever lives stands a greater chance of survival. Equally, if the brood is too big and the nest too small, she may make the difficult decision to sacrifice some of the hoglets to give the remaining babies a fighting chance.

But that doesn't explain hedgehog mothers eating their young if the nest is disturbed. One thought is that the mother makes a calculated call that if the babies are under threat from a predator, she may as well eat them first and gain the protein advantage. Another idea is that, under intense stress, the mother decides she can't cope with the immediate demands of hoglet-rearing and opts to abandon ship and start again elsewhere. In captivity, or if hoglets are well-meaningly handled in the wild, the scent of another animal – i.e. human – is also thought to confuse the mother, leading her to think that the babies are a food source.

# JULY

*It's July and the sky is cloudless. Gardens are parched and a blackbird sits listlessly on a lawn, its wings fanned out in the sun. Like a lido, there's a birdbath busy with visitors desperate to cool off; standing ankle-deep in water, sparrows and blue tits forget their differences and take turns dunking their heads down and forward to force the water down their backs.*

*In the countryside, rosebay willowherb blazes across verges and embankments in huge drifts. Its delicate, pink-purple flowers belie its success as an aggressive colonizer – especially on ground that's been catastrophically burned or destroyed. No wonder that after the Second World War it soon earned the name 'fireweed' or 'bombweed'.*

*On field margins and woodland rides, early July butterflies are on the wing (the purple emperor, silver wash fritillary and white admiral), while new adult ladybirds gorge themselves on aphids.*

*Down in the maternity nest, five hoglets have opened their eyes and the first tooth buds are starting to show. The mother is still feeding them herself, but next month it'll be time for the babies to leave the nest permanently. She has just a few weeks to get them weaned and not all her hoglets will make it through this difficult stage. For the*

*best chance of survival, she knows she has to*
*get them hunting for themselves. So, with*
*no time like the present, she ushers them out*
*into the darkness for their first*
*foraging trip...*

## Making Tracks

So, how do you know if you've got a hedgehog in your garden? If it's happy and healthy, you probably won't see it out in the daytime, but there are some clues to look out for that are a dead giveaway...

### POO

Hedgehog droppings look like thin black slugs – cylindrical, about 3–5 centimetres (1–2 in) long, and 1 centimetre (1/3 in) thick. In the wild, they're usually firm and packed with bits of shiny beetle shells (which can make the poo look slightly sparkly). The droppings of rescue hedgehogs, fed on pet food, tend to be squishier and dull (and very stinky).

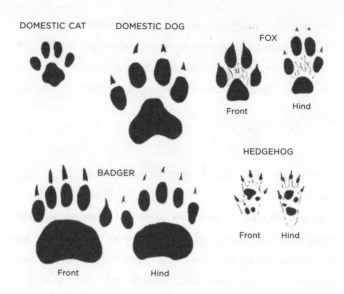

DOMESTIC CAT

DOMESTIC DOG

FOX

Front

Hind

HEDGEHOG

BADGER

Front

Hind

Front

Hind

## FOOTPRINTS

Hedgehog footprints look like children's tiny hand-prints. Both back and front feet have five toes – the front feet are slightly wider and the back feet slightly thinner and longer. The prints are about 3 centi-metres (1 in) wide and long, but unless the ground is very soggy the hedgehog won't often leave any marks. If you think you might have a hog wandering around at night, make a simple tracker at home by filling a baking tray with wet sand, putting some cat food in the middle of the tray, and seeing what's walked over the tray in the morning. Opposite are what hedgehog tracks look like... and a few others that might cross your path.

### NOISE

The best time to hear hedgehogs is during the mating season (May–June), when there's plenty of huffing and puffing going on. You might also hear the odd scuffle, as male hedgehogs fight over a female. The rest of the year (bar hibernation between December and March), go out at dusk or dark and you may catch the sound of hedgehogs rootling among the undergrowth or even finishing a meal – hedgehogs are noisy eaters, so listen out for gentle grunting, snorts, crunching and plenty of open-mouthed eating.

## *Help a Hedgehog No. 3*

### SICK OR INJURED HEDGEHOGS

As hedgehogs are elusive and nocturnal by nature, if you do find one out in the daytime it's fair to assume that something may be wrong. But not all hedgehogs out in daylight hours need human assistance and, in some cases, intervention may be worse than leaving well alone. On the following pages there's a quick flow chart to help you decide the best course of action, but if you're in any doubt, always err on the side of caution and phone a rescue centre or vet for advice (see Directory, page 131, for contact details).

### HOW TO HANDLE AN ADULT HEDGEHOG

When you are handling a hedgehog, always wear **gardening gloves**. Be gentle and quiet – hedgehogs hate loud noises and will flinch or curl up at sudden sounds. Either pick it up with both hands as a curled-up ball or, if it's uncurled, slip one hand gently under its tummy and lift.

Place the hedgehog in a large, high-sided **cardboard**

**box** or plastic storage box – they're fantastic climbers and escape artists, so make sure the box is either very deep or you have a lid with plenty of air holes. In the bottom of the box, put in a clean towel or thick layer of newspaper – hedgehogs are enthusiastic poo-ers and wee-ers.

If the hedgehog feels cold to the touch, you can place a **covered hot water bottle** in with it (touch the outside of the hot water bottle – if it's too hot for you, it'll be too hot for the hog). The temperature of the hot water bottle has to stay consistently warm – keep checking it and reheating the water. Make sure there's enough space for the hedgehog to move away from the hot water bottle if it gets too warm.

For baby hedgehogs, see Rescuing Orphaned Hoglets, page 63.

**If a hedgehog is in danger or distress – don't delay. Use the Directory at the back of this book to find your nearest rescue centre or call your local vet.**

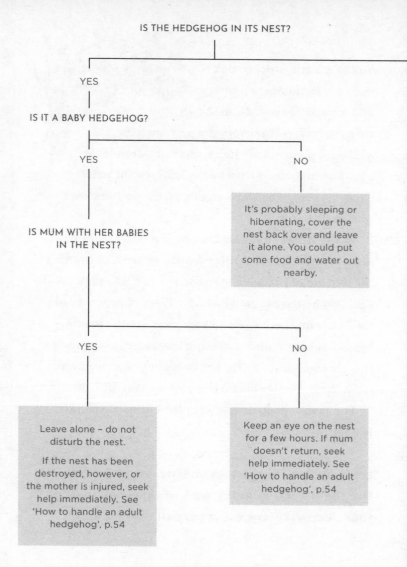

IS THE HEDGEHOG IN ITS NEST?

YES

IS IT A BABY HEDGEHOG?

YES

NO

It's probably sleeping or hibernating, cover the nest back over and leave it alone. You could put some food and water out nearby.

IS MUM WITH HER BABIES IN THE NEST?

YES

NO

Leave alone – do not disturb the nest.

If the nest has been destroyed, however, or the mother is injured, seek help immediately. See 'How to handle an adult hedgehog', p.54

Keep an eye on the nest for a few hours. If mum doesn't return, seek help immediately. See 'How to handle an adult hedgehog', p.54

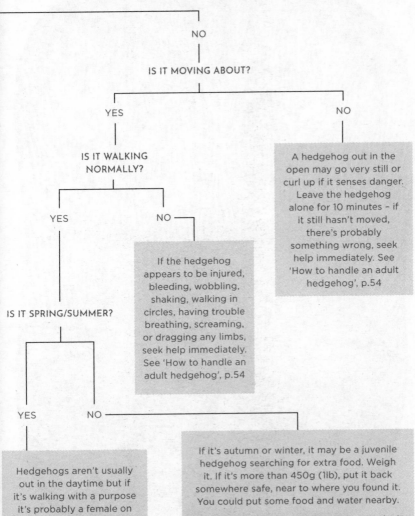

NO

**IS IT MOVING ABOUT?**

YES

**IS IT WALKING NORMALLY?**

YES

NO

**IS IT SPRING/SUMMER?**

YES

NO

NO

A hedgehog out in the open may go very still or curl up if it senses danger. Leave the hedgehog alone for 10 minutes – if it still hasn't moved, there's probably something wrong, seek help immediately. See 'How to handle an adult hedgehog', p.54

If the hedgehog appears to be injured, bleeding, wobbling, shaking, walking in circles, having trouble breathing, screaming, or dragging any limbs, seek help immediately. See 'How to handle an adult hedgehog', p.54

Hedgehogs aren't usually out in the daytime but if it's walking with a purpose it's probably a female on a foraging hunt or nest building. Put some food and water out and leave it alone.

If it's autumn or winter, it may be a juvenile hedgehog searching for extra food. Weigh it. If it's more than 450g (1lb), put it back somewhere safe, near to where you found it. You could put some food and water nearby.

If it's less than 450g (1lb) it might not make it through hibernation. Seek help immediately. See 'How to handle an adult hedgehog', p.54

# AUGUST

*July slides seamlessly into August. A week's worth of squally showers lift to reveal an unbroken run of sunny days. Combine harvesters are out in force, cutting vast swathes of barley and wheat before their good luck runs out; the pale stubbly fields, dotted with grain, become a free-for-all for scavenging birds.*

*Clouds of butterflies find themselves drunk on buddleia, its honey fragrance proving too delicious to resist. Grasshoppers, enjoying the dry spell, jump from stem to stem, stopping only to seesaw a quick song on their hind legs.*

*It's the month of finales. Crops are ready. Allotments burst. And hedgerows are heavy with ripe fruit; handful upon handful of blackberries, elderberries and dewberries are ready for the taking, if the blackbirds don't beat you to it.*

*Down in the burrow, the hoglets prepare to leave home for good. The wide world beckons, with all its dangers. One hoglet didn't make it back from a practice foraging trip and the rest will need to be on high alert – only half of the four hoglets that set out today will live through their first hibernation. But, at least for the moment, the weather's fine and there's plenty to eat. And so, without so much as a backward glance, the hoglets leave their home, mother and each other, unlikely ever to cross paths again...*

## Predators and Danger

Something is going wrong for hedgehogs. Despite the fact that they're one of the best-defended mammals in existence, their numbers are plummeting.

Wild animals in the UK that would deliberately target a hedgehog are few and far between. Birds of prey, weasels, stoats and foxes have all been known to attack hedgehogs but it's only the badger, with its powerful front claws, that makes a regular meal of the adult. The fact that hedgehogs and badgers have co-existed for thousands of years, however, without a significant decline in the former's numbers, suggests that most of the blame can't be laid on badgers' stripy shoulders.

Pets can be an issue – dog attacks are unfortunately common, especially in suburban areas, but cats tend to leave hedgehogs well alone once they've got the measure of their spines. Pet owners can help significantly in reducing hedgehog attacks, however, by putting their dogs on a lead if they're out at dusk or dark, when hedgehogs are most likely to be out.

The main danger for hedgehogs is, unfortunately, man. Our impact on the species isn't fully understood but it's fast becoming clear that our efforts to intensify agriculture, rip up wild spaces, increase development and overuse certain pesticides has had a catastrophic effect. If you remove the natural habitat of the hedgehog, i.e. the hedge, and poison or remove its food source, i.e. insects, it's a sure-fire recipe for disaster. Add to this the effect of roads and increases in traffic (which kill over ten thousand hedgehogs in the UK alone each year) and it's easy to see why the hedgehog is having a hard time.

## DID YOU KNOW

*Hedgehogs are fast runners in short bursts, reaching top speeds of 9km (5½ miles) per hour.*

# Help a Hedgehog No. 4

## RESCUING ORPHANED HOGLETS

Raising baby hedgehogs is a precarious business and it doesn't take much to disturb a nest. So if you accidentally destroy a nest in your garden or find an array of abandoned hoglets, what's the best course of action?

The first thing to mention is how to handle hoglets. If you are picking up **baby hedgehogs** it's vital you use gloves as your scent may cause the mother to panic and kill them. If they are still in the nest, pick it up in its entirety and place in a box. If the mother is also there, place her in a **separate box**.

Baby hedgehogs will also need to be kept warm. Place a **covered hot water bottle** in with the hoglets (touch the outside of the hot water bottle – if it's too hot for you, it'll be too hot for the hoglets). The temperature of the hot water bottle has to stay consistently warm – keep checking it and reheating the water. Make sure there's enough space for the babies to move away from the hot water bottle if they get too warm.

**If you're in doubt about whether to rescue or not, give your vet or local rescue centre a call first. They will be able to advise you on the best course of action. Don't try to look after baby hedgehogs yourself. They need specialist food, housing and knowledge if they're to stand any chance of survival.**

### THE NEST IS DISTURBED BUT MUM AND BABIES ARE SAFE

If you disturb a nest by accident but the mum and babies are fine, it's best to cover the nest back over again and leave well alone. You could put some extra food and water near the nest so she doesn't have to travel too far for nourishment.

### THE NEST IS DISTURBED BUT MUM ISN'T THERE

If you find a nest full of hoglets, mum may not be far away, so it's best to cover the babies back over and leave well alone. Monitor the nest for a few hours – if she doesn't return and the hedgehogs are starting to make loud peeping noises (which is telling you they are hungry) or they venture out of the nest, they'll need rescuing and taking to a vet or rescue centre (see Directory, page 131).

## THE NEST IS DISTURBED AND MUM IS DEAD OR INJURED

Adult hedgehogs often stay very still if they're scared and may be mistaken for dead. Even if mum looks very still, watch her for ten minutes. If she doesn't move, take her and the babies straight to a vet or rescue centre in **separate boxes** (the vet may want to establish cause of death). If she's very obviously injured, she'll need immediate attention. Again, take her and the babies in separate boxes.

## BABIES OUT OF THE NEST

If you find a baby hedgehog out of its nest in the day, by itself or with other hoglets, something's wrong. Look for others nearby – hoglets don't tend to come in single numbers. Take to a rescue centre or vet.

# Diseases and Parasites

Hedgehogs are infamous for being a bit, well, flea-y. And while it's true that many hedgehogs do carry **fleas**, it's perhaps less well known that hedgehog fleas (*Archaeopsylla erinacei*) are species specific and won't be in a hurry to jump onto the nearest cat, dog or human that crosses their path. (The hedgehog flea prefers widely spaced spines; human, cat and dog fleas like short, dense hair and fur.) Estimates vary on the number of fleas a hedgehog usually carries – many have none, lots have tens, and a sick hedgehog may have hundreds. Hedgehogs can also carry the odd **tick**, usually one of two species – the 'hedgehog tick' *Ixodes hexagonus* or the less fussy *Ixodes ricinus*.

It's difficult to know how bothersome either fleas or ticks are to their prickly hosts. Most hedgehogs seem to bumble along quite happily with the odd parasite but it's interesting to note that sickly hedgehogs are often heavily infested with either fleas or ticks. It's tricky to know which comes first – is the sickly hedgehog an easy target for parasites or are the parasites making the hedgehog poorly? Either way, the relationship is deeply damaging and needs immediate treatment.

It's not a job for an amateur, however. Conventional pet medicines such as dog flea sprays or Frontline can be deadly for a hedgehog – you'll need to take it to a vet or rescue centre who'll have an array of hog-friendly treatments on hand.

Hedgehogs also suffer from a number of other common diseases, all of which are treatable if caught in time but lethal if left to develop: **lungworm,** which is common over autumn and winter, causes coughing and respiratory distress; **ringworm,** which can lead to fur and spine loss, skin lesions and scratch wounds; and **flystrike,** a particularly nasty problem,

DID YOU KNOW

*Hedgehogs usually live around 3–7 years in the wild but the oldest recorded example was a female who lived to the ripe old age of 15, in captivity in Germany.*

prevalent in summer, when flies lay tiny eggs that hatch into skin-eating maggots. If you find a hedgehog with any of these symptoms or signs, take it to a vet or rescue centre immediately.

## *Help a Hedgehog No. 5*

### THE HEDGEHOG-FRIENDLY GARDEN

Gardens are full of promise and possibility for the average hedgehog. Mixed perennial planting, deciduous trees and vegetable plots attract huge numbers of delicious insects, while garden sheds, compost heaps and leaf litter are all tempting places to grab forty winks. There are, however, plenty of places where an unsuspecting visitor could come a cropper – from garden netting to slug pellets, ponds to poisons – so here's how to create a safe haven for hogs.

| HEDGEHOG FRIENDLY | HEDGEHOG UNFRIENDLY |
|---|---|

## Build a bug hotel

It might seem a little cruel to build a hotel for guests you hope will get eaten, but attracting invertebrates into your garden – such as beetles, spiders and centipedes – will provide a valuable supply of food for a hungry hedgehog and help keep other insect pests at bay.

## Slug pellets

Three problems with slug pellets: first, you're reducing the hedgehogs' food supply; second, hedgehogs are poisoned by eating slug pellets; and third, hedgehogs are also poisoned by eating dead or dying slugs that have been treated. **Use natural slug control methods such as egg shells and beer traps.**

## Have a compost heap

Decaying organic matter is full of invertebrates and makes for a cosy nesting place for hedgehogs. If you need to empty your compost bin, do it in April – after hibernation ends but before the breeding season – or late in October, when nests are empty. If you're turning a heap, check for signs such as droppings or burrowing holes, or have a quick rummage with your hands first.

## Netting

Plant supports, garden netting, football nets, electric fencing – hedgehogs regularly get tangled and die in all kinds of plastic and wire garden mesh. **Reduce your use of netting, store it out of harm's way when you're finished and keep plant netting 30 cm (12 in) off the ground. If a hedgehog gets entangled, don't try to pull it out. Cut around the netting and take the hedgehog and netting to the vet, who can carefully untangle it and treat any wounds.**

| HEDGEHOG FRIENDLY | HEDGEHOG UNFRIENDLY |
|---|---|
| **Plant bug-friendly plants** | **Ponds & pools** |

**Plant bug-friendly plants**

Create a wildlife haven and you'll find insects will flock to your garden. Many of these will be beneficial to your garden and provide a hearty meal for hedgehogs. Get your garden buzzing with a mixture of flowering plants such as fennel, wild marjoram, English lavender, yarrow, scabious, ornamental thistles and honeysuckle.

**Ponds & pools**

While it's good to have a water supply for wildlife, ponds with steeply sloping sides and swimming pools are deadly for hedgehogs and any other animals that tumble in. Hedgehogs can swim, but not for long. **Make sure any pond or pool has at least one gently sloping side or a ramp as an escape route.**

**Attract more worms**

Hedgehogs love earthworms. They're also important for the health of your soil. Encourage earthworms to flourish by spreading rotting organic material such as compost, dried leaves or manure along your beds. These provide a ready food source for earthworms, a source of nutrients for your soil and, in turn, the odd snack for a hungry hedgehog.

**Bonfires**

A log pile or stack of branches is a tempting nesting site for a tired hedgehog. **Always check a bonfire before lighting – use a broom handle, not a fork, to lift up the base of the bonfire and look for signs for life. Better still, remake your bonfire before you light it.**

| HEDGEHOG FRIENDLY | HEDGEHOG UNFRIENDLY |
|---|---|

## Put a hole in your fence

Hedgehogs need to roam huge distances to find enough food to eat – one garden is not enough. Solid fences between gardens stop hedgehogs moving through their natural territories so make sure you cut a small hole 13 x 13 cm (5 x 5 in) at the base of your fence or, better still, use hedges as boundaries instead. See Creating Hedgehog Highways page 87 for more information.

## Strimmers & mowers

Strimmers and other garden machinery cause unimaginable injuries to hedgehogs, which are often sleeping or foraging in long grass. **Before you strim, spend just a few minutes going over the area with a soft broom, checking for wildlife, especially under any hedges or shrubs and in patches of tall weeds or grass.**

## Create nooks and crannies

Wildlife often likes damp, cool, quiet places; make a friendlier garden by adding rock piles, wood stacks, leaf litter, compost heaps, drystone walls, sheds or log stores, shallow ponds, climbing plants such as ivy or clematis, native trees and wild patches.

## Timber preservative

Hedgehogs are fascinated by new smells and tastes, and will often lick freshly applied creosote or other toxic preservatives and paints. **Look for brands that are non-toxic and pet-friendly.**

# SEPTEMBER

*It's early September and the countryside
is letting off the last of her fireworks.
Gardens burst with mature colour – deep
burgundies, flares of purple and spikes
of hot pinks – with verbena, nigella
and sedums all keeping the bees and
butterflies happy.*

*On these last few stolen sunny days, autumn
seems a million miles away, but in just a few
weeks the last of the flowers, and good
weather, will have faded into the
background.*

*For careful foragers, there's still a bounty of
rich pickings – rosehips and late blackberries
in the hedgerows, carpets of blue whinberries
up on the moors, and a store-cupboard's
worth of sweet chestnuts, hazelnuts
and beechnuts.*

*The young hoglets, with a month of
independent living under their belts, are
fattening up quickly. It's vital they make the
most of these mild, late summer days –
the period between now and December is
a frantic grab to gain enough weight to carry
them through hibernation. But time is
on their side – they've still got weeks to go
until the really hard weather starts
to bite.*

*But it's not so easy for any newly born
hoglets. Some hedgehog mothers have
managed a second litter in late August
or early September. Others have mated later
than usual and only just given birth. For
these late arrivals, the clock is against them.
Once the babies have been weaned it'll
be October and, for many, there's just not
enough time or food to reach hibernation
weight. For these 'autumn juveniles',
it's a race against time...*

## Hedgehogs and Ecology

A species shouldn't have to justify its own survival.
And yet, when it comes to hedgehogs and many other
quiet creatures of the countryside, it seems that some
people don't understand what all the fuss is about.
What's one or two fewer hedgehogs between friends?
Does it matter that numbers have declined rapidly ?

People are genuinely fond of hedgehogs – they're a
popular icon of the countryside – but few have got to

75

grips with just how significant they are to our environment and why it matters if they disappear.

For humans, hedgehogs are very effective pest controllers. Their voracious appetite for creepy crawlies, and the astonishing volume of insects they can consume in one night, lightens the load for a frustrated gardener and negates the need for any expensive, toxic chemicals such as slug pellets. They're also brilliant scavengers – chomping up dead mice, chicks and other unfortunates – the clearer-uppers of the ecosystem, who not only tidy away carrion but recycle it as nutrients into the ecosystem.

Hedgehogs are also the 'canary in the mine' when it comes to the wider environment. The decline in hedgehog numbers has rung alarm bells about the health of our countryside; if hedgehogs are disappearing due to lack of food and fragmented habitat, what does it say about the state of our soils or the future of pollinating insects? And if hedgehogs don't have enough places to breed or sleep, what can we deduce about the way we manage our hedgerows, fields and natural spaces moving forward?

But perhaps, more than all of this, what does the hedgehogs' decline say about our relationship with nature? If we can let our 'favourite' animal slip into obscurity and we fail to save the hedgehog – an animal so embedded in our culture and affections – it surely doesn't bode well for creatures who we don't feel any sentimental attachment for. Getting people engaged with hedgehogs, and caring about their progress, not only has a benefit for one species, but has a knock-on effect for other wildlife and the wider ecosystem.

# OCTOBER

*For most of the countryside, October
marks a gentle slowing down. Against
the backdrop of golds, browns and russet
reds, many creatures are packing up
for the forthcoming winter, hoping to
ride out the worst of the weather in
a warm, safe corner.*

*While some insects won't make it any further than these few weeks, some are hardier or have developed strategies to get through the colder months. Dark sheds, tree bark and dense climbers become safe havens for overwintering insects such as ladybirds and herald moths. Underground, buried alone in soil, a new queen bumblebee stays safe, leaving the old queen and the rest of the hive to perish outside.*

*And down in the woodland, a badger is preparing its sett, ready to hunker down. Come the snow, it'll be cosy – the family will huddle together in a blanket of bracken and dried leaves – dad, mum and a handful of youngsters not yet ready to leave home for good. There'll be the odd foraging excursion if a mild night presents itself – but for most of the next few months there'll be little else to do but snooze.*

*For the solitary hedgehog, however, there'll be no family reunions. Hibernation isn't far*

around the corner and her mind is solely
focused on foraging. The worsening weather
has meant many of her favourite insects are
nowhere to be seen but there are still plenty
of earthworms and slugs to root out, hidden
among the wet leaves and decaying
vegetation. With any luck, she might find
a dead mouse, mole or baby rabbit on her
night-time travels – every calorie she takes
on now will increase her chances of
outlasting the winter. At this late stage,
a hearty meal of carrion tips the balance
in her favour...

## Help a Hedgehog No. 6

### HELPING AUTUMN JUVENILES

Hedgehogs born late in summer are playing a deadly
game of catch-up. Most hoglets – who will arrive in
June – will have weeks to fatten up in time for hibernation but those born in September or early October
often struggle to reach a decent weight. For these

'autumn juveniles', the outlook can be bleak – those who hibernate underweight may use up their fat reserves before the mild weather returns and starve. For those who don't hibernate, the search for food is often fruitless, especially when the temperature plummets.

But you can help. If you find a hedgehog between October and February, the first thing to do is put on some garden gloves, pick it up and **weigh it**.

If the hedgehog weighs **less than 300 grams** (10 oz), it may not even be weaned yet – these hoglets need immediate specialist assistance. Keep it warm with a hot water bottle (see Rescuing Orphan Hoglets, page 63) and take it straight to a rescue centre or vet.

If it's **between 300 and 450 grams** (10–16 oz) it's probably an autumn juvenile and will need extra feeding before hibernation or, in some cases, bringing inside and overwintering. Take to a rescue centre or vet.

If it's **between 450 and 600 grams** (1–1¼ lb), it is recommended that the hedgehog is left to hibernate as it is very likey to survive. In this instance, speak to your local rescue centre or vet – they will be able to give you advice based on local weather conditions and time of year. If you are advised to leave the hedgehog alone, you can still put food and water out for it – hedgehogs often make short excursions during hibernation and these top-up meals can be life-savers.

If a hedgehog is **over 600 grams** (1¼ lb), leave it to hibernate as rescue could actually do more harm than good. Again, put water and food out nearby. You could also provide some nesting material or a ready-made house (see Making a Hedgehog House page 97) if the hedgehog hasn't built its hibernaculum yet.

Regardless of weight, if you find a hedgehog between October and February out in the **daytime** and it appears **unwell or injured**, it'll need taking to a rescue centre or vet.

# City Hedgehogs

We reached a point, a few years back, when more of the world's population lived in urban areas than the countryside. Wildlife is having to adapt. For some creatures, like the urban fox, the city offers a handful of lucky breaks – a place where scavenging opportunities are plentiful and outweigh the risks from traffic and human contact. For others, like the hedgehog, the picture is a little more complicated.

There are, however, reasons to be cautiously optimistic. Recent research showed that hedgehogs can happily live in city parks and urban gardens, but only under certain conditions. Finely manicured lawns and sterile bedding plants don't offer anything to urban hedgehogs – they need natural bushy areas and wild vegetation, places where insects thrive and hedgehogs can hide unseen from humans and pets.

Urban gardens and parks, unlike farmed land, are often surprisingly biodiverse, with plenty of mixed planting, trees and vegetables that attract a variety of creepy crawlies. Cities are more than just buildings – even in urban areas, about half of all land is still classed as 'green space' (things like allotments, parks, back gardens, verges, patches of woodland and so on), so there's still a huge potential resource for hedgehogs to draw on. The key, however, is to allow hedgehogs the opportunity to travel safely between these green spaces. It's not complicated – often as simple as cutting small, hedgehog-sized holes in garden fences – but the results are profound (see Creatin Hedgehog Highways page 87).

Urban householders often leave food outside – either accidentally or deliberately – and hedgehogs can and do exploit this free resource. Rubbish bins, litter, food scraps, pet food, bird tables – there are plenty of places an urban hedgehog can grab a quick snack. And this perhaps explains why urban hedgehogs don't seem to travel as far as their country cousins in the course of a night's foraging, covering

a range of just 5 hectares (12 acres) versus the usual 20 (50 acres) for a rural hedgehog (on average adult hedgehogs travel between 1–2 km per night over home ranges as big as 10–20 hectares in size).

But city life isn't easy. Traffic is a huge cause of hedgehog mortality even though research has also shown that urban hedgehogs usually wait until human activity quietens down before they come out to forage. Many stay hidden until well after midnight, coming out much later than they would in the wild, therefore making the time they have for foraging much shorter for urban hedgehogs. It's also

interesting that, despite having access to plenty of food all year round, city hedgehogs still choose to hibernate, making it even more imperative that they have quiet, undisturbed wild areas even in the busiest of town centres.

## *Help a Hedgehog No. 7*

### CREATING HEDGEHOG HIGHWAYS

Hedgehogs need space. One garden is not enough. We know that they travel huge distances for food, but they also need to roam far and wide to find a suitable mate (if they don't, they run the risk of interbreeding). In the countryside, this isn't too tricky; but in densely populated urban areas, where gardens are fenced off from each other, it can be impossible for a hedgehog to navigate its way through.

We know that one of the reasons for the hedgehog's decline is its inability to access large tracts of land. By removing or altering the physical barriers between gardens, we can change this situation for the better. And it couldn't be easier.

- **Cut a hole in your fence**
  Cut a hole, at ground level, the size of a CD case
  (13 x 13 cm/5 x 5 in). Sand off any rough edges.

- **Dig a tunnel**
  If you don't want to cut a hole, scrape away a
  channel of earth so the hedgehog can slip under
  the fence.

- **Create a passage**
  If you have a solid wall, use a core drill to create
  a passageway or remove a loose brick. Or use
  a short length of soil pipe to create a tunnel
  through a wire fence.

- **Replant with a hedge**

  If a new boundary is needed, consider a hedge instead. These allow hedgehogs to come and go freely (and provide places for them to sleep) but also bring in other wildlife and garden-friendly insects.

- **Build any new fences off the ground**

  If you need a new fence, install it with a 13 centimetre (5 in) gap at ground level.

- **Get the rest of the street involved**

  Encourage your neighbours to do the same – the more gardens you can link together, the bigger the range your local hedgehogs will enjoy.

**N.B. Garden boundaries are often shared, so check with your neighbours first.**

# NOVEMBER

*It's early evening and the night promises
to be a cold one. Come the morning, it'll
be misty – the November dew condenses
during the night – but for now, the skies
are black with starlings, flocking en masse
before roosting in the darkness. From the
ground below, it's a hypnotizing sight –
their diving, swooping and sudden changes
in direction matching any aerial display.*

*Blustery showers and hard frosts strip the trees of their remaining colour. Piles of crunchy, curling leaves might spoil the park-keeper's day but for many creatures leaf litter is late-autumn's lifeline. The leaves, twigs and small shreds of bark provide valuable cover for nature's minibeasts such as snails, worms and spiders, who'll wait out the winter in this gradually decomposing sanctuary.*

*For the hedgehog, November's leaf litter is not only a store-cupboard, filled with delicious insects, but also a source of building material for the nest she'll start to construct. Over the next week or so, she'll carefully build her 'hibernaculum' or winter nest, using leaves, bracken, twigs, grass or straw pulled from nearby.*

*Trotting backward and forward with mouthfuls of dry material, she steadily pieces together a cosy retreat, taking care to choose a site that's well hidden but warm.*

*For the urban hedgehog, nesting under a
compost heap or shed is often the only
option, but out in the open countryside,
she'll find a brambly hedge or
abandoned burrow.*

*Just a few more trips to the leaf pile and her
nest is complete. Once inside, like a dog in its
bed, she pads round and round in circles,
'combing' and flattening the interior until
there's space for her to curl up. Eyes closed,
her heart rate slows and, in no time,
she's drifted off into a very deep sleep...*

## Hibernation

Actually, to call hibernation 'sleep' is wrong. Far
from being a prolonged snooze, hibernation is a much
more involved and genuinely miraculous process.

The first question to ask is: why bother to hibernate
at all? For the hedgehog, there are two compelling
reasons: first, during a harsh winter, food is thin on

the ground. Many of the things that hedgehogs love to eat, such as insects, small mammals and birds' eggs, either die, hide or simply don't exist over the coldest months; and second, it takes a lot of energy to keep a hedgehog warm. Remember that somewhere deep in their evolutionary past, hedgehogs swapped fur for spikes. Great for defence. Not so great when it's freezing outside.

So hedgehogs developed an ingenious strategy. Rather than struggle through the snow and ice, spending more energy searching for food than they could recoup, hedgehogs decided to wait the winter out. But they don't just hide somewhere warm. To use up as little energy as possible, hedgehogs enter a state of suspended animation. (We don't know why, but the male hedgehogs tend to go into hibernation earlier than the females, and also come out of hibernation sooner in the spring.) It's also interesting that in northern New Zealand, where hedgehogs were introduced in the late 1800s and enjoy warmer year-round temperatures, hedgehogs don't feel the need to hibernate.

Amazing physiological changes happen: their body temperature plummets from their usual 34°C to a chilly 2–5°; they stop breathing, or at least their respiratory rates drop from between 25 and 50 breaths a minute to barely breathing at all, instead cycling through long sessions of not breathing at all, followed by quick bursts of rapid breaths; the heart slows drastically – from a pacy 150-ish beats per minute to a moribund 10 or so bpm. In fact, almost every part of the hedgehog's physiology slows down during hibernation.

In this state, the hedgehog can live off its internal stores of fat for months. During the hibernating weeks, the hedgehog wakes up occasionally – sometimes in response to a change in the outside temperature or because their nest has failed in some way. A hedgehog may also rouse for an extra foraging trip, and it seems that most of the energy used up over the winter is during these short forays. Either way, it's only a brief spell of wakefulness and the hedgehog will soon slip back into her torpor. From the outside, the hedgehog can appear lifeless. She's cold to the touch and doesn't move, but tap her

gently or make a sudden sound and she may uncon-
sciously respond, her spines slowly moving or gently
tightening her curled body further.

For hibernation to be successful, it's important
that the nest is a constant temperature. Too cold and
the hedgehog may freeze to death. Too warm and the
hedgehog might use up her valuable fat reserves too
quickly or wake up wrongly, assuming it's spring. It's
vital, therefore, that the hibernaculum is well protected from the outside temperature. Most nests are
brilliantly insulated and match the hedgehog's own
hibernation temperature of between 2 and 5°, even
when it's well below freezing or unseasonably mild
outside.

Only when spring arrives, and the outdoor temperature is a consistent 10–12°C or so, will the
hedgehog emerge from her nest. Waking up from

such a deep 'sleep' takes anything from a few hours to half a day, as the hedgehog's circulation, breathing and body temperature gradually return to normal. Waking up from hibernation is a slow process. Eyes closed, the hedgehog stays very still until its body reaches 20°C. Then, partially awake, eyes now open, it shivers and staggers around with drunken gait until it nears its goal of 34°.

During her long period spent in the nest, she'll have lost around 30 to 40 per cent of her body weight – the first few weeks after hibernation ends are, not surprisingly, a focused search for food and a race to get back to a weight that will let her mate and breed when early summer comes.

## *Help a Hedgehog No. 8*

### MAKING A HEDGEHOG HOUSE

Hedgehogs use three different types of nests during the year: their summer nests, the nursery nest and the hibernaculum. While each nest varies in its construction – for example, the hibernating nests are more substantial than the loosely pulled-together summer nests – access to leaves, grass and other building materials can be a real issue for a hedgehog who needs somewhere to stay.

Building a hedgehog house (or buying a ready-constructed one – see Directory, page 131) provides a safe, warm space for a hedgehog to sleep, give birth or hibernate. Leave it in a quiet corner of the garden, and it will house successive hedgehogs – who might stay for just one night or hunker down for weeks over winter.

The following pages show you how to construct a simple one of your own.

Once the house is built, here's where to place it in your garden:

- Somewhere quiet, where it won't be disturbed by passing feet, pets or wheelie bins. Against a wall, fence or under a hedge or bush is ideal.
- Face the entrance of the house away from the prevailing wind/rain.
- Place the house near plenty of nesting material – the hedgehog will want to build her

own nest, so site the box next to lots of leaves, straw, hay, grasses or fine twigs. The more unkempt and hidden, the better.

- Once it's in place, don't be tempted to peek – you can tell if the house is occupied by leaving a few leaves in the entrance of the house and seeing if they've moved after a few days. Assume over winter that the house is occupied.

- If it's looking like a particularly harsh winter, you can protect the box (leaving the entrance uncovered) with a layer of plastic sheeting and place a thick covering of leaves over the entire house for extra insulation.

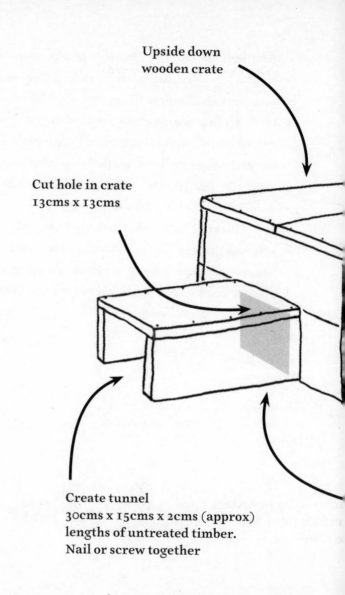

**Upside down wooden crate**

**Cut hole in crate 13cms x 13cms**

**Create tunnel 30cms x 15cms x 2cms (approx) lengths of untreated timber. Nail or screw together**

Paint the entire box in a
non toxic pet-friendly wood
preservative or varnish

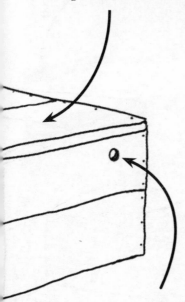

Cut second hole
for ventilation

ail or screw tunnel
er hole from inside of
e crate

# DECEMBER

*It's December and most of the creatures
that preoccupy the hedgehog are nowhere
to be seen. It's been a bitterly cold run-up
to Christmas and the garden snails have
crawled into nooks and crannies to bed
down for winter. They'll seal themselves
off – literally – from the outside world,
using their silvery mucus to brick up
the entrances to their shells until the
warm weather returns.*

*The hum of insects has also been silenced. Most of the butterfly population will spend winter as larvae, but a handful attempt to brave it out as adults – the peacock, comma and small tortoiseshell settling in abandoned barns and outbuildings until the spring. The earthworm – also seeking sanctuary from the cold – has abandoned the surface soil and headed deeper underground to find any trace of warmth.*

*Dormice are asleep. In fact, they've been hibernating since late October and will spend months snoozing away most of autumn, winter and early spring. Named after its propensity for napping (the word 'dormouse' coming from the Old French dormir, 'to sleep'), this little creature will hibernate, like the hedgehog, but wait even longer to emerge. Despite his tiny size, he can spend up to three-quarters of his life asleep – fattening up quickly over summer before he takes to his bed again.*

*And all is quiet in the hedgehog hibernaculum. Despite the rapid drop in temperature at night-time, the inside of the nest stays constant – it looks as if the hedgehog's meticulous nest-building and those extra layers of insulating leaves are starting to pay dividends...*

## Hedgehogs and Humans

Humans are strange creatures. We can love an animal to distraction, obsess over it, sentimentalize it, make it the subject of childhood stories and national pride and yet, in the same breath, be immune to its plight.

If you unpack the relationship between people and hedgehogs over the years, it's not always been an easy one. From the earliest written texts that feature hedgehogs, it seems they've been misunderstood. Pliny,[1] writing only a few decades after the birth of Christ, talked with great confidence about hedgehogs catching food by impaling it on their spines:

*They wallow and roll themselves upon apples and such fruit lying under foot, and so catch them up with their prickles, and one more besides they take in their mouth, & so carrie them into hollow trees.*

Medieval manuscripts continue the error – the 12th-century Aberdeen Bestiary[2] describes

*The hedgehogs, covered in bristles, roll up in a ball, and carry grapes back to their young by impaling them on their spines.*

It seems no one had bothered to actually watch a hedgehog at work.

Perhaps such misunderstandings could be forgiven by the fact that hedgehogs are nocturnal, their habits rarely seen in the daytime. But scroll forward a few years and the hedgehog meets a whole new level of ignorance.

The Destruction of Crows, etc. Act, passed by Henry VIII in 1532, and the subsequent Preservation of Grain Act of 1566 were drawn up in response to a series of catastrophic harvests. The edict was simple – everyone must catch and kill as many grain-munching 'vermin' as they can and, in return, they'll be paid handsomely for their troubles. Each creature on the 'hit list' had a bounty on its head – a penny for a kite to twelve pence for a fox – despite the fact that many of the animals on the list had absolutely no interest in eating grain. Few native creatures escaped the slaughter – kingfishers, adders, crows, badgers, woodpeckers, polecats, weasels, sparrows,

wild cats and, of course, the hedgehog.

Villages and towns that failed to kill enough wildlife were fined. The prospect of punishment, combined with the generous rewards paid for every dead creature presented to the parish, meant that, over the next two hundred years, populations of native birds and mammals were decimated, some to the point of near extinction. Over half a million bounties were paid for culled hedgehogs alone between the 16th and 18th centuries.

The hedgehog has also had the unfortunate luck of being, apparently, delicious. Evidence from Neolithic sites suggest that hedgehogs were regularly eaten – possibly wrapped in grasses or clay and then roasted in an open fire – and there are worryingly specific recipes for hedgehog, served every which way, throughout history. One medieval book from 1425 describes a dizzying meal consisting of as many animals as you could wish to find in a children's book: from deer to peacock, cranes to curlews and, of course, the poor old hedgehog.[3]

A 19th-century account of Romany gypsy life by George Borrow[4] writes 'These children sometimes bring home "hotchiwitches", or hedgehogs, the flesh of which is very sweet and tender, and which their mothers are adepts at cooking', and even as recently as the Second World War, hedgehogs provided a valuable source of foraged food. 'WW2 People's War', an archive of wartime memories compiled by the BBC, describes how Italian POWs showed Suffolk villagers the secrets of catching and cooking wild food during lean times:[5] 'I remember summer evenings when they'd catch rabbits and cook them with us. They would also catch hedgehogs. They'd gut them, roll them out and make fires in the earth. The hedgehogs were rolled up in clay and baked in the ashes. Then the Italians would hit the clay off and the prickles would come off with it and then they'd eat the meat with bread.'

Thankfully, hedgehogs are no longer considered meaty treats or foraging fodder. Thanks to the Wildlife and Countryside Act (1981), it's illegal to kill or capture wild hedgehogs using certain methods, and under the Wild Mammals (Protection) Act

(1996) they're also protected from cruel treatment. So, while you're not going to be arrested for running over a hedgehog by accident, if you're caught trying to teach a hedgehog a lesson with a crossbow you're going to be in some serious trouble.

Keeping a wild animal as a pet is also illegal, but there's a grey area when it comes to keeping a hedgehog that's been injured. As it stands, you don't need a licence to rehabilitate a hedgehog – i.e. look after it until it's well enough to be released – but this may well change in the future to ensure that rescue centres and well-meaning individuals meet some kind of minimum welfare requirements.

# JANUARY
# &
# FEBRUARY

*Winter has ticked by slowly. By the end of February, there's hope that the weather has done its worst and spring is just around the corner. It's an unpredictable time, however. Cold snaps and snow drifts can come at any time, and often as late as April, but it doesn't stop the snowdrops and aconites spreading, carpet-like, under the trees – always the first flowers to break through winter's grey gloom.*

*Chaffinches, blackbirds and song thrushes sing the new year in. A fat-bellied mistle thrush, out on the woodland floor, chatters loudly. He's a bold, pompous songster – happy to sing however harsh the weather – earning himself, in days gone by, the nickname 'storm cock'.*

*One bird who doesn't need to croon, however, is the great spotted woodpecker. Come February and you'll hear him drumming on tree trunks, his stiff tail feathers acting as a prop as he clings to the bark and hammers away with his powerful beak. It's a distinctive sound – only a few seconds long, around ten beats, fading out at the end; rather than singing a song to claim his territory, his rapid pounding lets other woodpeckers know that this patch of woodland is taken.*

*And down in the hibernaculum, the hedgehog's enforced isolation is nearly at an end. In just a few weeks she'll wake from her*

*slumber, hungry and much thinner, but*
*ready to start the year's cycle all over again.*
*With any luck, she'll mate again and have*
*another litter of hoglets in early summer. She*
*won't get many bites of the cherry – in the*
*wild, hedgehogs rarely live longer than three*
*or four years – but, who knows, given some*
*extra food during lean times, plenty of room*
*to roam and a warm place to sleep, she could*
*enjoy as many as ten summers in her*
*lifetime. That, however, is down to you…*

## Hedgehogs and Literature

Literature has been kind to the hedgehog, poets and writers finding the hedgehog's indefatigable spirit and impish charm worthy of a few lines. In the ninth century, Chinese poet Chu Chen Po[6] wrote, with admiration:

> *He ambles along like a walking pin cushion,*
> *Stops and curls up like a chestnut burr.*

*He's not worried because he's so little.*
*Nobody is going to slap him around.*

In one ancient tradition, the hedgehog is a hero. The story goes that the Devil, having smuggled himself onto Noah's Ark, tries to sink the boat by boring a hole in the hull. The hedgehog saves the day, and scuppers the Devil, by stuffing his prickly body in the hole.

Shakespeare also mentions the hedgehog or 'urchin'. For him, it's a creature of impish spirit, not altogether benign but worthy of respect. In *Macbeth*, the 'hedgepig' is one of the witches' familiars; in *A Midsummer Night's Dream*, the fairies' spell insists that 'thorny hedgehogs are exorcised' and in *Titus Andronicus*, Tamora explains with dread, 'A thousand fiends, a thousand hissing snakes, Ten thousand swelling toads, as many urchins, Would make such fearful and confused cries' (it's interesting that naughty children are still called 'urchins'). In fact, hedgehogs pop up all over Shakespeare – from *Richard III* to *The Merry Wives of Windsor*. Even *The Tempest* gives the hedgehog a mention, as Caliban describes his torment 'then like hedgehogs which Lie tumbling in my bare-foot way and mount Their pricks at my footfall'.

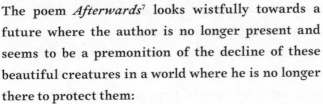

One of our greatest poets, Thomas Hardy, also wrote about the hedgehog – although not in the happiest of circumstances. The poem *Afterwards*[7] looks wistfully towards a future where the author is no longer present and seems to be a premonition of the decline of these beautiful creatures in a world where he is no longer there to protect them:

> *If I pass during some nocturnal blackness,*
> *mothy and warm,*
> *When the hedgehog travels furtively over the*
> *lawn,*
> *One may say, "He strove that such innocent*
> *creatures should come to no harm,*
> *But he could do little for them; and now he is*
> *gone.*

But no one did more to secure the nation's affection for the hedgehog than Beatrix Potter. *The Tale of Mrs Tiggy-Winkle* (1905), a hedgehog washerwoman, is undoubtedly the most successful story about a hedgehog ever written and transformed how the public viewed a creature previously regarded with some suspicion. Mrs Tiggy-Winkle was industrious, fastidious, and just a little shy – traits we still associate with the hedgehog today. What's interesting to note, however, was the heavy streak of nostalgia that also ran through the book – describing an unchanging, idyllic picture of the countryside that was at odds with the rapid industrialization of the land. It's interesting that, even then, there was a sense that rural life was changing perhaps beyond recognition and the hedgehog was a symbol of the bucolic dream.

Few people realize that the inspiration for Mrs Tiggy-Winkle came from Potter's own pet hedgehog, which travelled alongside her. In one of her many letters, Potter writes: 'Mrs. Tiggy as a model is comical; so long as she can go to sleep on my knee she is delighted, but if she is propped up on end for half an hour, she first begins to yawn pathetically, and then she *does* bite! Nevertheless, she is a dear person; just like a very fat rather stupid little dog. I think the book will go all right when once started.' Sadly, while the book was a hit, life on the road for a wild hedgehog proved too much. Only a few months after the book was published, Mrs Tiggy falls ill. In a moment of rather typical Victorian stoicism and practicality, Potter swiftly chloroforms the hedgehog and buries it in the back garden. They don't tell that ending to children.

## Do Hedgehogs Make Good Pets?

It's clear that Mrs Tiggy made a better muse than a pet. In fact, even Beatrix Potter herself admitted that she was 'afraid that the long course of unnatural diet and indoor life is beginning to tell on her. It is a wonder she has lasted so long.' Wild hedgehogs don't make good pets – they hate being handled, only come out at night, eat voraciously and, as one would expect, poo copiously. It's also illegal to take a hedgehog from the wild as a pet, so that knocks that one on the head.

But what about other species of hedgehog? African Pygmy hedgehogs (APH) are a much smaller breed and have, in recent years, become something of a craze, both in the UK and the United States. It's not hard to see why – they're unbelievably cute. Responsible APH owners know just how much care needs to go into looking after a domesticated hedgehog and therein lies the problem – many folks who buy APH don't know what they're letting themselves in for.

As with all hedgehogs, they're shy, solitary creatures – certainly not the right pet for a busy, noisy family environment. Most hedgehogs don't enjoy being picked up or stroked and those that do still need careful handling, especially with such spiky spines – again, not a good pet for kids. Some APH will adapt to a different routine but their natural state is to be up and active at night (not ideal if you share a room with one) and wherever you keep the cage, it'll need to be cleaned out regularly and scrupulously.

If you do want to keep a hedgehog as a pet, it's important you know the level of commitment involved and only buy one from a reputable breeder. It's worth noting that, in some US states, it's either illegal to own a hedgehog or you need to obtain a permit – always check first.

As with all pets, many people buy one in a hurry and then realize they don't have the time or patience to look after it. Increasing numbers of APH are being dumped or released into the wild, which presents a number of problems, not least for the tiny hedgehog. APH are exotic animals and cannot tolerate cool weather. Even in warmer countries, the release of an exotic animal may have consequences for native species in terms of either predation or disease.

It can be tricky, however, to tell a native European hedgehog from an African pygmy hedgehog (APH), especially in the juvenile stages.

If you see a hedgehog out in your garden that has the following features, it may be an exotic species that'll struggle to survive unless it's brought indoors

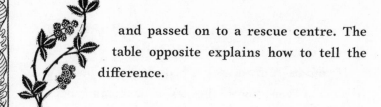

and passed on to a rescue centre. The table opposite explains how to tell the difference.

## Help a Hedgehog No. 9

### HOW TO GET INVOLVED

There are, thankfully, lots of people who love hedgehogs and want to help. By following all the 'Help a Hedgehog' advice in this book, you're making a difference and giving hedgehogs a better chance in the long term. If you're keen to do more or volunteer your time, however, there are a number of ways you can get actively involved.

### FIND A RESCUE CENTRE NEAR YOU

There are hundreds of rescue centres across the country – some are run by individuals, others as a group venture. Either way, they're often keen for volunteers to help care for sick or injured hedgehogs. Use the Directory on page 131 to find your nearest centre and see if they need an extra pair of hands.

|  | EUROPEAN HEDGEHOG | EXOTIC HEDGEHOG |
| --- | --- | --- |
| Colour | Usually dark brown with creamy-brown belly fur (although you can get albino wild hedgehogs with white spines and fur and pink eyes) | Usually white furry belly with black and white banded quills and dark markings on face. There are lots of variations in colour, however, from 'salt and pepper' (very dark) to cinnamon (very pale) |
| Size | Large – around 25 cm (10 in) long as adults and weighs between 450 g and 1.2 kg (1–2½ lb) | Small – around 12.5–20 cm (5–8 in) as adults and weighs between 200 and 600 g (7 oz–1¼ lb) |
| Feet | Large feet, long toes and claws (to help them dig in the soil) | Tiny feet and toes (more used to scavenging than digging) |
| Ears | Small ears, not prominent | Large ears, prominent |

N.B. If you do think you've found an exotic hedgehog, or you're in any doubt, take it to your nearest rescue centre or vet.

## DONATE, JOIN, SUBSCRIBE

All wildlife charities struggle for income. Some cover a broad range of animals, such as The Wildlife Trust or Tiggywinkles, while others focus their attention solely on hedgehogs, such as The British Hedgehog Preservation Society. Such organizations rely on donations or membership to keep up their valuable work. Join up, donate, subscribe – it all goes towards vital research and front-line care.

## FUNDRAISE

If you're brilliant at raising money, why not choose a hedgehog charity as one of your causes? Whether you run the PTA at your local school, bake cakes for a summer fete, organize a drinks party or do something sponsored on your own initiative, a one-off fundraiser is a great opportunity not only to raise money but also to introduce a large number of people to the issues involved. Online fundraising websites, such as justgiving.com, can take your fundraising idea national or even international.

## SET UP A DONATION PLATFORM

Raising money for a good cause can be as painless as registering with an online platform such as easy-fundraising.org.uk. Sites like these donate money to your good cause – in this case, hedgehogs – every time you or one of your supporters shop online at an approved retailer. Donations usually range from 1 to 5 per cent of every purchase, or they'll give you a lump sum on a service purchase such as car insurance.

## BECOME A HEDGEHOG CHAMPION

Most people don't have a clue that hedgehogs are in decline. One of the most powerful things you can do to effect change is to read up, get informed and start passing on this information to anyone who'll listen. Give a talk to your local Women's Institute, U3A or primary school, arrange a village hall meeting about how the community can help, tell friends, family, neighbours and colleagues. Join in with initiatives such as HedgehogStreet.org, where you can gain access to free resources such as posters, leaflets, action cards and slides for a hedgehog-themed talk. Spread the word.

## GO SOCIAL

Social media is a valuable tool when it comes to raising awareness. If you want to get other people passionate about hedgehogs, set up a Twitter account or Instagram feed and start posting. Photos and short videos often garner more attention than words alone. Use them to tell a narrative or highlight a particular issue, such as hedgehogs and Bonfire Night, and encourage followers to share your advice.

If you're out and about helping hedgehogs, take photos of your behind-the-scenes work, whether it's a talk at a village hall or a day spent volunteering at a rescue centre – authentic 'in the field' footage always gets lots of attention, likes and comments. Follow other people who are interested in helping hedgehogs – there's a wide community out there. Use #hashtags effectively – they'll help your searchability.

# NOTES

1. *The Eighth Booke of the Historie of Nature*,
   C. Plinius Secundus

2. The Aberdeen Bestiary, Folio 24R, University of
   Aberdeen

3. *Antiquitates culinariae*, R. Warner (1791)

4. *Romano Lavo-Lil: Word-Book of the Romany
   or English Gypsy Language*, G. Borrow

5. Hedgehogs and Bread by Hadleigh Community
   Event: http://www.bbc.co.uk/history/
   ww2peopleswar/stories/50/a3181150.shtml

6. 'Hedgehog' by Chu Chen Po (9th century), trans-
   lated by Kenneth Rexroth, from *100 More Poems
   from the Chinese*. Copyright © 1970 by Kenneth
   Rexroth. Reprinted with the permission of New
   Directions Publishing Corporation

7. 'Afterwards', Thomas Hardy (1840–1928)

# DIRECTORY OF RESOURCES

HEDGEHOG WELFARE, INJURIES OR ILLNESS

### British Hedgehog Preservation Society

Tel: 24-hour helpline 01584 890801 or
visit www.britishhedgehogs.org.uk

### Tiggywinkles

Tel: 24-hour helpline 01844 292292 or
visit www.sttiggywinkles.org.uk

### RSPCA

www.rspca.org.uk

### Animal Rescuers

www.animalrescuers.co.uk

## FURTHER INFORMATION ON HEDGEHOG HABITAT, WILDLIFE & CONSERVATION

### Hedgehog Street

A joint campaign run by the People's Trust for
Endangered Species and the British Hedgehog
Preservation Society (BHPS)
www.hedgehogstreet.org

### The Wildlife Trusts

www.wildlifetrusts.org

### People's Trust for Endangered Species

www.ptes.org

### The Mammal Society

www.mammal.org.uk